OH, MY WORD

*The insanely simple 5-minute daily journal to
intentionally become who you want to be*

CHERYL WILSON-STEWART

ILLUSTRATIONS BY CLAIRE MOORE

OH, MY WORD
Copyright © 2019 by Cheryl Wilson-Stewart

Tellwell Talent
www.tellwell.ca

ISBN
978-0-2288-1740-6 (Hardcover)
978-0-2288-1739-0 (Paperback)

THIS JOURNAL BELONGS TO...

Brenda E (Krammes) Miller
1-25-22 70th Birthday
gift From Steve, Jeanette,
Seleah and Jathan
Seitzinger

OH, MY WORD

Brendoo's Famous Phrase!

Today is the day to *intentionally* choose who
you want to be and how you want to live

*Your greatest self has been waiting your
whole life; don't make it wait any longer.*

~ Steve Maraboli

For those who want to live
every day with joy.

Table of Contents

Welcome Friend,

Just for fun.

Close your eyes. Take a deep breath.

See yourself as the person you've always wanted to be living the life you love.

As the images form, your heartbeat slows.

An inner smile escapes gently, curling the corners of your mouth.

A feeling you realize you haven't felt in a while tickles your insides.

Could it be ... *joy?*

You want to freeze this moment.

Exhale. *"Aaaaaaaahhhhhhh ..."*

Then you open your eyes.

And you're transported back to the chaotically anxious world where you feel overwhelmed and stressed. Worry and negative thoughts fill your mind. You catch a glimpse of yourself in the mirror and wonder, *"Who is that?"*

If this sounds familiar, you're in good company. In today's world, most of us struggle with feelings that hold us back from being who we want to be and living a life we love.

Just last week, I was leading a workshop, and a woman walked in, holding her head as if it was about to explode, and pleaded, *"I need SOMETHING to change my life. I've got five minutes a day. Is this going to help me?"*

"Yes, sister, it will!" I said. I've been there, and here's my story.

For almost as long as I can remember, anxiety had been my very annoying and disabling sidekick. If you've experienced this, you know it's like being held hostage by your own negative thoughts that loop around and around, becoming the loudest voices in your head. After trying many strategies to break the loop, I thought this was just my lot in life. My family and friends simply accepted me as this tightly wound, anxious person.

But this was not who I wanted to be.

Then I started doing what I called "heart doodles." This was a simple, relaxing activity in which I would write and colour an inspiring word or phrase on a blank index card. During the day, my mind would flash on the card and I would remember the word. Good feelings would flood through me.

I still have the first heart doodle I created six years ago. I drew a big heart and wrote the word joy inside. I found some pencil crayons (probably my daughter's leftover school supplies) and went to town. I remember feeling a childlike sense of joy as I coloured and made my little masterpiece come to life. I posted my doodle on the bulletin board facing my desk, a happy, colourful, visual reminder of who I wanted to be. Every time it caught my eye, I'd smile and feel a little internal *aaaahhh*.

I doodled more.

I eventually became a disciplined heart doodler, spending five minutes every morning *intentionally* choosing a word representing who I wanted to be or what I wanted to bring into my life before creating my mini-canvas.

It wasn't long before I realized the noisy loop of anxiety wasn't demanding my attention. It had been drowned out by positive thoughts that filled my head as well as feelings of joy, peace and fulfillment that bubbled from the inside. I wasn't engaged in a daily struggle, and I wasn't fixated or clinging to a negative thought. Instead, an inner peace had moved in. For what felt like the first time in my life, I was in the driver's seat, choosing the thoughts I wanted to think.

It's often said that when we can boil something down to its simplest form, we achieve mastery. I'd found a way to banish anxiety and worry, make what I wanted to think the loudest voice in my head and feel joy on a daily basis *and* it was OH. SO. SIMPLE.

I later found there was a scientific basis for the increased joy, fulfillment and sense of control I was experiencing. I was rewiring my brain. I was reprogramming and reconditioning my mind and my life.

The good news is you don't have to be in a laboratory to do this work. You can do it from the comfort of a cozy chair with a cup of coffee.

So, I ask you, dear reader, what would your life be like if you knew exactly how to use your thoughts to influence your reality and allow you to feel more joy and become the person you wanted to be?

Got the juices flowing? I hope so.

My goal is for you to find in this journal a five-minute strategy that will put a smile on your face, help you change your life in extraordinary ways and bring you the joy and fulfillment you crave.

With love,

5

HOW IT WORKS

Each day is a blank canvas. You are the artist, the author, the driver, the creator of your life. By choosing an intention for the day and bringing it to life on the page, you are rewiring your brain. With your thoughts, you are creating the person you want to be and the life you dream of. This intention will help put worry and anxiety to rest and clear away blocks in your conscious and subconscious mind. Negative thoughts will be replaced with those of joy, peace and fulfillment. This method of journaling is simple and powerful and will make you feel great right from day one.

The journal has three daily sections:

1. A new, inspiring quote to uplift you and help you focus your thoughts.
2. A five-minute morning ritual when you choose an intention, draw or write the word(s) and then make it colourful with pencil crayons, gel pens, glitter or whatever excites you.
3. An Evening Reflection question ends your day with gratitude, a joyous heart and ready for sleep.

BENEFITS

The *OH, MY WORD* method of journaling has changed my life in so many positive ways. I even discovered there was a sound scientific basis (more on that to come) as to why and how it worked. Here are a few of its benefits:

- Helps you to stop settling for less than you truly deserve, start living as the person you want to be and creating the most awesome life you can imagine
- Lowers stress
- Rewires your brain to think in new ways and creates new neural pathways
- Makes your positive, intentional thoughts the loudest voices in your head
- Allows you to interrupt your negative thoughts and replace them with positive ones
- Sets the tone for the whole day when done first thing in the morning
- Helps you focus on what is truly important by getting rid of the clutter and surprisingly you are more productive
- Allows you to choose every day who you want to be, how you want to express yourself and how you want to live—you are in control
- Creates a visual history of your intentional journey that you can look back on
- Gives you an easy and fun way to make big changes in your life that takes five minutes a day

OH, MY WORD

PILLARS

THOUGHT
Every thought
you think creates
your reality.

CHOOSE
You choose who
you will be in every
moment of every day.

INTENTION
Intention is the
catalyst for any
change you desire.

TODAY
Today is where
your power is.

Thought

Never underestimate the power of your thoughts—they create your reality. In fact, with each of the 60,000 to 70,000 thoughts we think every day, we are actively creating our future. The problem is the majority of these daily thoughts are the voices of fear, doubt, worry and anxiety and are recycled from the day before and the day before that and the day before that. We infuse these thoughts with an enormous amount of emotional energy, and as a result they become the biggest, loudest and most powerful thoughts in our head.

That doesn't bode well for today or the future, does it?

We need a way to replace the negative, nagging thoughts with those representing the highest intentions of who we are and want to be. It's not that we don't have these positive thoughts—we do. It's just that they're busy navigating the 1,000-lane thought expressway, battling thousands of blaring thought streams while attempting to generate energy and gain momentum.

It's a tough go for these intentional thoughts. You can see how the highest expression of who we are, what we want and how we want to live our lives might get lost in the chaos.

The good news is that we, as the creator of our lives, can crank up the volume by becoming clear on what we want, choosing an intention and moving it from thought to action every morning.

To activate, our intentions need fuel to move from our head into our heart. This fuel supply is provided by the emotions and allows for the integration of body and mind, where the real magic happens.

THE SCIENCE BEHIND OH, MY WORD

When we understand something intellectually (in the left side of the brain) and then make it "experiential" by moving it into our emotions (in the right side of the brain), we are providing the life-giving fuel our intentions need for liftoff. This happens when we draw and colour the intention word. It is then we can think and *feel* the thought. When we experience the thought, we can change.

This experiential process actually rewires the brain, causing the neurons to create new patterns and producing a chemical that the body remembers as we move through the day.

We're also creating what scientists call "thought interruption," in which the new positive thought interrupts the negative, disempowering thought that was demanding our attention and disables it. The positive super-charged intentional thought then powers through the congestion and gets to work.

"DRAWING" ON EVEN MORE SCIENCE

A recently published study in *Current Directions in Psychological Science* by researchers at the University of Waterloo in Ontario, Canada, found that drawing has a "surprisingly powerful influence" when used as a tool to help the retention of information in the memory, something the researchers have dubbed the "Drawing Effect."

Scientists also tell us the act of taking deliberate action, such as making a drawing, creates the energy needed to move the intention (or thought) into the prefrontal cortex of the brain, where it is able to move from thought to action. Bingo!

THE REWIRED BRAIN

When you do the simple five-minute OH, MY WORD daily ritual, it alters the brain, causing the neurons to start firing in new ways. The mind remembers your intention and is on the lookout for ways to manifest and make it concrete.

You think it. Feel it. Live it.

You are actively creating who you want to be by using a single word.

Choose

Whether you realize it or not, you choose your life every day.

Although you don't necessarily choose the circumstances, you do choose—consciously or unconsciously—the person you are going to be.

When you consciously choose who you are going to be and how you are going to live, every day is filled with opportunity to savour, change or redirect course.

Every day you choose the direction and the habits that will lead to your best life.

What a privilege. What an honour. What an opportunity.

Intention

Life gets a lot simpler when you clear the thoughts that make it complicated and replace them with intentions that reflect your highest ideals and who you want to be. It is here you can change your life and create a new state of being.

Living with intention is like using maps to chart your destinations instead of allowing the winds of chance to haphazardly blow you from place to place. You choose the route and all the stops you will make along the way. You are in the driver's seat with your hands on the wheel. In this place, intentions point you towards the person you've always wanted to be while living a deeply fulfilling life.

When you begin living with intention, your life starts to change. It's subtle at first: a sense of feeling good and looking forward to the day. Then you notice a definite shift as positive thoughts are filling your mind and you notice you are expressing yourself differently.

It's happening … you are becoming who you want to be.

Today

I am sure you remember the expression *"Today is the first day of the rest of your life."* It was popular years ago and was used to commemorate *every* life passage imaginable.

I don't know about you, but I eventually came to think of it as a cute, well-used expression that had its day.

But I was missing something.

Life is a series of "todays" one after another after another from the time we're born until we die.

The todays become the days, weeks, months and years that strung together become our life.

While today may not be the *first* day of your life, it's unquestionably the most important one and where your power is. It is where every dream you have begins to form and where you choose who you are and how you're going to live. Today is a clean canvas, a new beginning, a fresh opportunity.

Want to peek into your future? Look at today.

Years ago, I asked my blog readers, *"What do you want from life?"*

There were many responses: *I want my life to have meaning and purpose; I want to wake up excited about the day; I want to feel fulfilled; I want to leave a mark; I want to feel joy; I want to be happy; I want to help others; I want to love and be loved.*

It would stand to reason that when you know what you want from life, you know what needs to happen and when. That makes today the most important day of your life.

So how can you make the most of it?

It's simple. Today, start by choosing your intention.

What will it be?

All. Up. To. You.

We don't stumble accidentally into a wildly fulfilling, deeply satisfying, jaw dropping life. We create it.

~ Marc and Angel

The Daily Ritual

Got five minutes? That's all it takes to experience more joy and make your life the masterpiece it deserves to be. Here's everything you need to know to create a daily ritual that can change your life.

The journal has 90 daily pages—that's three months of intentionally choosing who you want to be and how you will live. To inspire you, I provide 130 possible intentions in six important categories. Every morning, you're provided with a quote to focus your thoughts and a mini-canvas where you will draw and colour your chosen intention.

Lastly, you are provided a thought-provoking Evening Reflection question at the bottom of each daily page. There are 65 of these questions. You can use these questions to gain insight on the day, express gratitude and prepare for a restful sleep.

This daily ritual has you covered from morning to night, and it's so simple. Here are the steps:

1. **READ** the quote on the left of the page to give yourself a boost and focus your thoughts.
2. **CHOOSE AN INTENTION,** either one word or a short phrase, from the list or create one of your own.
3. **COMPLETE THE SENTENCE** *"Today I choose to . . ."* with your chosen intention that describes who you most want to be or how you want to live today.
4. **DRAW THE WORD** or write it over and over, filling the page.
5. **COLOUR IT!** Spend five minutes making it beautifully colourful using pencil crayons, gel pens, crayons or glitter. You can add images or symbols. Have Fun. Be playful. There is no right or wrong way to do this—only *your* way.
6. **EVENING REFLECTION** Read the question and respond with the first thought that comes to mind.

That's all there is to it. Your intention has been put into action.

As you go through the day, your mind will remember the intention, your body will feel it, and you will live it. Your Evening Reflection will close the day with positive thoughts.

Goodnight.
Sweet Dreams.

Choosing An Intention

How do you choose an intention when the list of possibilities is infinite? I've got you covered. To get started, I've given you 130 intentions to choose from that represent six important areas of your life. As you read through the word lists, you might find yourself wanting a little bit of everything, like wanting to taste all the flavours at an ice cream shop because they all look so good! Luckily, there are two super simple and very effective ways to approach your intention selection and narrow it down to the one that is right for you today.

1. Get quiet, close your eyes and ask yourself <u>one</u> of the following questions:

   What do I need today? What could I use more of in my life? What characteristics or qualities do I choose to cultivate in myself today? Who do I want to be? How do I want to feel? How do I want to express myself? Don't overthink this. Relax and go with what first comes to mind.

2. Look over the intention word lists and see what pops out.

Words contain energy. You're looking for an intention word or phrase that carries a "charge" for you. The charge will present as a stomach flutter, an internal "yes" or a simple knowing it is the intention you unconsciously need or are looking for. When you choose an intention word, not only are you empowering it to be the guiding principle of the day, but you have become an active participant in the creation of your life. You've set the tone for everything that follows.

Today is the day to start becoming the person you want to be and creating the life you love. What could be more exciting than that?

SUPERCHARGING AN INTENTION

Super charging an intention is fast, easy and fun. There are two simple steps. Choose an intention for the day (an intellectual process) and then draw and colour the word in your journal (an experiential step), devoting five minutes to bringing it to life on the page.

Seriously, that's all there is to it.

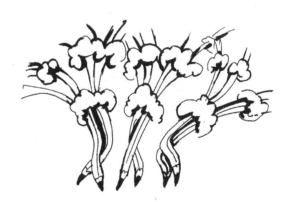

The Intentions

Intentions are very personal and touch every aspect of life. They represent who you want to be, how you want to express yourself and how you want to live. As you explore the intentions that follow, you will *feel* those that have power for you.

The intentions are broken down into six important areas that most of us crave for a rich, fulfilling life. You may want to focus solely on one area for a period of time or choose daily intentions representing all the areas. The only thing to remember is that it's impossible to make a mistake! You will benefit from choosing any intention from these lists.

It's time to get excited about the possibilities. Let go of any limitation you've had and see yourself as the person you've always wanted to be. Here's the key to unlock the door. You *can* become the person you always knew you were capable of becoming and living the life you've dreamed of. Insert the key and open the door. I'm excited to see how your life will change.

Here are 130 intentions to be inspired by.

You are perfectly cast in your life. I can't imagine anyone else in the role. Go Play.

~Lin-Manuel Miranda

Physical Well-Being

Today I choose to ...

Radiate

Focus

Rest

Recharge

Breathe

Heal

Move

Celebrate

Be Healthy

Be Free

Be Surprised

Be Peaceful

Love Myself

Give Thanks

Show Appreciation

Nourish my Body

Work up a Sweat

Life Balance

Today I choose to ...

Meditate

Laugh

Dream

Share

Dance

Simplify

Shift

Reset

Play

LOOSE

RESET RESET RESET

play

Listen
Appreciate
Pause
Be Mindful
Hang Loose
Curl Up
Let Go
Slow Down
Make My
Heart Sing
Clear the Clutter

Emotional Fulfillment

Today I choose to ...

Cherish

Love

Embrace

Soften

Become

Unfold

Emerge

Connect

Nurture

Be Worthy

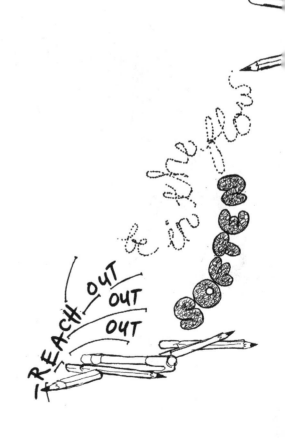

Be Vulnerable
Be Enough
Be Grateful
Be Courageous
Be Willing
Be Present
Be Joyful
Be Hopeful
Be in the Flow
Reach Out
Follow My Heart

Spiritual Growth

Today I choose to ...

Believe

Trust

Surrender

Pray

Listen

Seek

Discover

Understand

Question

Receive

Forgive

Serve

Love

Search

Awaken

Have Faith

Be Transparent

Be Present

Be Silent

Be Still

Be Authentic

Be Compassionate

Go Inward

Live in Grace

Open My Heart

Listen to My Inner Voice

Creative Expression

Today I choose to ...

Explore

Begin

Recover

Challenge

Create

Experiment

Learn

Expand

Grow

Observe

 follow my own path

Be Fearless
Be Inspired
Be Uncomfortable
Be Curious
Say Yes
Open My Eyes
Step Outside My Comfort Zone
Stand Up for What I Believe in
Speak My Truth
Do Something that Scares Me
Try Something New
Follow My Own Path

Success And Achievement

Today I choose to ...

Start
Learn
Prosper
Conquer
Finish
Dream
Be Creative
Be Unforgettable
Be Optimistic
Be Disciplined
Be Dedicated

Be Accountable

Be Unstoppable

Be Fearless

Be Honest

Be Limitless

Seize Every
Opportunity

Go for It!

Take a Risk

Refuse to Settle

Go Forward

Do the Right Thing

Ask Questions

Challenge Myself

Walk on the Edge

Sample Journal Pages

Here are a few pages from my own journal. I wish you could see them in colour because that's when intentions truly come to life. You'll have to use your imagination.

When I begin, I don't know how the page will look.

I choose my word and put pen to paper.

Then I colour ... *and* ...

SURPRISE!

It pops right off the page.

Throughout the day I 'see' my word and 'feel' the emotion.

The intention has become the loudest voice in my head, and I am becoming the person I want to be.

Date: June 30

Today I choose to...

FOCUS
FOCUS
FOCUS
FOCUS

Evening Reflection:
What discovery did I make today?

I discovered I could be in charge of my thoughts and that when they get
chaotic and scrambled it was because I let them. A-Ha!

Date: April 24

Today I choose to...

listen listen listen listen
listen listen listen listen
listen listen listen listen
listen listen listen listen

 listen

listen listen listen listen
listen listen listen listen
listen listen listen listen

Evening Reflection:
What happened today that came as a complete surprise?

I heard things today that are still rolling through my mind. I think I miss a lot! Will try to listen twice as much as I speak.

Date: March 14

Today I choose to...

Evening Reflection:
What do I want to remember about today?

I let my true self show in all I did and said. Once I got into it, it became easier. I CAN do this.

Date: December 3

Today I choose to...

SURRENDER

Evening Reflection:
What was memorable about today?

Mid way through the day I realized I wasn't holding myself rigid and tight.
I felt calm and peaceful and light. I was afraid of surrendering. Not now.
Need more.

Date: May 10

Today I choose to...

Evening Reflection:
Three words to describe how I felt today.

Free ... Excited ... Strong

Date: January 24

Today I choose to...

Evening Reflection:
What did I do that made me smile today?

Whenever my mind told me, don't do that, you might fail or people might laugh ... I pushed through anyway. Go. For. It. Didn't hurt. Need to make this my intention more often.

Frequently Asked Questions About The OH, MY WORD Method

An important part of bringing OH, MY WORD to you was to assemble a group of people willing to test the daily ritual in their own lives and offer feedback and comments. These are the FAQs that helped them make the most of OH, MY WORD

What kind of art supplies do I need?

I like to outline my word with a black gel pen while others prefer a graphite pencil. My personal favourite tool for colouring is pencil crayons although crayons and coloured gel pens work well. Stay away from markers and paint as they will bleed through the paper.

Can I spend more than five minutes a day working in my journal?

Five minutes is all it takes to make the journaling process effective for most people. However, you can spend as much time as you like!

Do I have to have a new intention every day or can I repeat?

You can repeat intentions until you see and feel the intention active in your life. The important thing is to spend at least five minutes every day creating a new page. In my journal, "*surrender*," "*let go*" and "*breathe*" have appeared more times than anything else. One woman happily reported using the same intention every day for two months. After that, she moved on to a new one.

Can I make up my own intentions or do I have to use the suggested ones?

Use whatever resonates with you. The suggested ones are just that, "suggested" intentions to get the wheels turning and illustrating the simplicity you're aiming for. You're looking for an intention that triggers a little power surge within. When it happens, you'll feel it. Go with that.

Are some intention words better than others?

Some words can be more powerful than others. Verbs tend to be effective as they are active and are showing you "how" to live. Intentions that embody a state of being (such as be courageous, be creative) also work very well. Ultimately whatever speaks to you and resonates with you is the "right" choice.

What if my mind is already spinning with overwhelming thoughts when I sit down to choose my intention?

I know how difficult these days can be. You feel inclined to skip the daily ritual and jump right into your day, ready to start sorting through all those thoughts. These are the days you most need to take five minutes and center yourself with intention. Even if negative thoughts are blocking the positive ones, choose a word like "breathe" and get it on the page. Reminding yourself to return to breath in stressful times is a chance for the body to reset and an opportunity for a new beginning.

What if my intention does not become the loudest voice in my head and negative thoughts take over? When this occasionally happens to me, I take deep breaths from the diaphragm and allow for long, slow exhales through the mouth. This calms my mind and body. Then I remind myself that I'm OK and every day is a new opportunity to begin again.

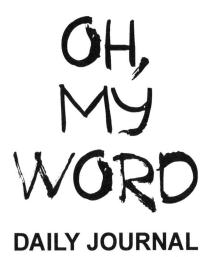

OH, MY WORD

DAILY JOURNAL

*It's time to start living
the life you've imagined.*

~ Henry James

Intentions compressed into words enfold magical power.

~ Deepak Chopra

Date:

Today I choose to...

Evening Reflection:

What was amazing today?

Dream and give yourself
permission to envision a You
that you choose to be.

~ Joy Page

Date:

Today I choose to...

Evening Reflection:

What surprised me today?

The thoughts we choose to think
are the tools we use to paint
the canvas of our lives.

~ Louise Hay

Date:

Today I choose to...

Evening Reflection:

What did I see today that I'm grateful for?

Let today be the day you give up who you've been for who you can become.

~ Hal Elrod

Date:

Today I choose to...

Evening Reflection:

What magical moment did I experience today?

An intention is a clear signal
we really want to change, and it
represents the result we want.

~ Dr. Joe Dispenza

Date:

Today I choose to...

Evening Reflection:

What did I feel today that I'm grateful for?

Today is a blank page in your life history. What will you write in it?

~ Sonya Parker

Date:

Today I choose to...

Evening Reflection:

What was meaningful to me today?

Life isn't about finding yourself.
It's about creating yourself.

~ George Bernard Shaw

Date:

Today I choose to...

Evening Reflection:

What is a moment from today I can celebrate?

Don't let the old you make your decisions. Today is the only day change exists. Change today and your entire life will be altered. Don't change today, and tomorrow will be exactly like today, forever.

~ Ariel Banayan

Date:

Today I choose to...

Evening Reflection:

What was better today than yesterday?

Make today worth remembering.

~ Zig Ziglar

Date:

Today I choose to...

Evening Reflection:

What do I want to remember about today?

It's not what you say to everyone else that determines your life. It's what you whisper to yourself every morning that has the greatest power.

~ Marc & Angel

Date:

Today I choose to...

Evening Reflection:
What did I touch today that I'm I grateful for?

How you start your day is how you
live your day. How you live your
day is how you live your life.

~ Louise Hay

Date:

Today I choose to...

Evening Reflection:

What happened today that I wasn't expecting?

Don't underestimate the power of thoughts and words. What you tell yourself every morning will set your mind and life on that path.

~ Nina Bolivares

Date:

Today I choose to...

Evening Reflection:

What brought a smile to my face today?

It is never too late to be what you might have been.

~ George Eliot

Date:

Today I choose to...

Evening Reflection:

What six words describe today?

We become what we think about.

~ Earl Nightingale

Date:

Today I choose to...

Evening Reflection:

What are three thoughts that
made me smile today?

Every intention sets energy
into motion, whether you're
conscious of it or not.

~ Gary Zukaf

Date:

Today I choose to...

Evening Reflection:

I learned something new today ... what was it?

Every morning you have two choices:
Continue to sleep with your dreams
or wake up and chase them.

~ Unknown

Date:

Today I choose to...

Evening Reflection:
What lit me up today?

Every intention is a trigger
for transformation.

~ Deepak Chopra

Date:

Today I choose to...

Evening Reflection:

What challenge am I grateful for today?

The only person you are destined to become is the person you decide to be.

~ Ralph Waldo Emerson

Date:

Today I choose to...

Evening Reflection:

What excited me about today?

I now know that nothing in my life will change until I change the way I see my life and myself.

~ Iyanla Vanzant

Date:

Today I choose to...

Evening Reflection:

What one thing gave me a boost today?

Be yourself; everyone else
is already taken.

~ Oscar Wilde

Date:

Today I choose to...

Evening Reflection:

What brought me joy today?

If you want a new outcome, you will have to break the habit of being yourself and reinvent a new self.

~ Joe Dispenza

Date:

Today I choose to...

Evening Reflection:

What made me laugh today?

The way we think about ourselves
will give rise to the world we live in.

~ Gregg Braden

Date:

Today I choose to...

Evening Reflection:

What did I hear today that I'm grateful for?

At the center of your being you have the answer; you know who you are, and you know what you want.

~ Lao Tzu

Date:

Today I choose to...

Evening Reflection:

How was today different than yesterday?

Your beliefs become your thoughts,
Your thoughts become your words,
Your words become your actions,
Your actions become your habits,
Your habits become your values,
Your values become your destiny.

~ Mahatma Gandhi

Date:

Today I choose to...

Evening Reflection:

There is always strength in the deepest places.
Where was the source of my strength today?

Once you make a decision, the universe conspires to make it happen.

~ Ralph Waldo Emerson

Date:

Today I choose to...

Evening Reflection:

What made me feel most alive today?

A person is only limited by
the thoughts they choose.

~ James Allen

Date:

Today I choose to...

Evening Reflection:

What did I do today that brought me happiness?

When you make a choice,
you change the future.

~ Deepak Chopra

Date:

Today I choose to...

Evening Reflection:

What surprised me today?

*You are the master of your destiny.
You can influence, direct, and control
your own environment. You can make
your life what you want it to be.*

~ Napoleon Hill

Date:

Today I choose to...

Evening Reflection:

What idea did I have today that I am grateful for?

There are far, far better things
ahead than any we leave behind.

~ C.S. Lewis

Date:

Today I choose to...

Evening Reflection:

What was memorable about today?

If you have good thoughts, they will
shine out of your face like sunbeams
and you will always look lovely.

~ Roald Dahl

Date:

Today I choose to...

Evening Reflection:

What do I cherish about today?

The biggest adventure you can ever take is to live the life of your dreams.

~ Oprah Winfrey

Date:

Today I choose to...

Evening Reflection:

What do I want to remember about today?

Yesterday is gone; tomorrow
has not yet come. We have
only today. Let us begin.

~ Mother Teresa

Date:

Today I choose to...

Evening Reflection:

What did I see today that made me smile?

The journey of a thousand miles
begins with a single step.

~ Lao Tzu

Date:

Today I choose to...

Evening Reflection:

What discovery did I make today?

The secret of change is to focus
all your energy, not on fighting
the old, but building the new.

~ Socrates

Date:

Today I choose to...

Evening Reflection:

What happened today that I did not expect?

Every morning we are born
again. What we do today
is what matters most.

~ Buddha

Date:

Today I choose to...

Evening Reflection:

Today is a projection of the future. What memory from today do I want to keep?

I am the one I have been looking for.

~ Iyanla Vanzant

Date:

Today I choose to...

Evening Reflection:

What filled me with gratitude today?

An intention synchronistically organizes its own fulfillment.

~ Deepak Chopra

Date:

Today I choose to...

Evening Reflection:

What was a moment from today that was pure joy?

Inside of you exists pure joy, pure bliss and profound inner peace. Everything you seek is already within you. The key is to get silent and feel what's inside.

~ Brittany J. Trumble

Date:

Today I choose to...

Evening Reflection:

What did I see today that I am grateful for?

*I'm really enjoying how my
life is beginning to unfold.*

~ Abraham Hicks

Date:

Today I choose to...

Evening Reflection:

What three words describe how I felt today?

I promise myself I will enjoy
every minute of the day that
is given to me to live.

~ Thich Nhat Hanh

Date:

Today I choose to...

Evening Reflection:

What happened today that came
as a complete surprise?

You are born with wings. Why
prefer to crawl through life?

~ Rumi

Date:

Today I choose to...

Evening Reflection:

What made me smile today?

If you are trying to build
something or become something,
write it, mean it, own it.

~ Unknown

Date:

Today I choose to...

Evening Reflection:

What new thing did I learn today?

We are constantly invited
to be who we are.

~ Henry David Thoreau

Date:

Today I choose to...

Evening Reflection:

What gave me hope today?

We cannot become what we want
by remaining what we are.

~ Max Depree

Date:

Today I choose to...

Evening Reflection:

What made me laugh today?

Don't look back; you're
not going that way.

~ Unknown

Date:

Today I choose to...

Evening Reflection:

What did I smell today that I am grateful for?

He who conquers others is strong; he
who conquers himself is mighty.

~ Lao Tzu

Date:

Today I choose to...

Evening Reflection:

What made me feel connected today?

Today, I create a wonderful new day and a wonderful new future.

~ Louise Hay

Date:

Today I choose to...

Evening Reflection:

What was most memorable about today?

At any moment, you have a choice,
that either leads you closer to your
spirit or further away from it.

~ Thich Nhat Hanh

Date:

Today I choose to...

Evening Reflection:

What can I celebrate from today?

Conscious thoughts, repeated often
enough, become unconscious thinking.

~ Joe Dispenza

Date:

Today I choose to...

Evening Reflection:

What did I do today that made me smile?

I believe in the person
I want to become.

~ Lana Del Rey

Date:

Today I choose to...

Evening Reflection:

What do I want to remember about today?

There is no passion to be found playing small — in settling for a life that is less than the one you are capable of living.

~ Nelson Mandela

Date:

Today I choose to...

Evening Reflection:

What was the lesson in today?

What you seek is seeking you.

~ Rumi

Date:

Today I choose to...

Evening Reflection:

What did I bring into my life today?

Some pursue happiness,
others create it.

~ Anonymous

Date:

Today I choose to...

Evening Reflection:

What was the magic today?

The secret to changing your life is in your intentions. Wishing, hoping and goal setting cannot accomplish change without intention. What is needed is a shift from inert energy of wanting to the active energy of doing and intention.

~ Wayne Dyer

Date:

Today I choose to...

Evening Reflection:

What did I discover today?

The happiness of your life depends
on the quality of your thoughts.

~ Marcus Aurelius

Date:

Today I choose to...

Evening Reflection:

What happened today that was amazing?

Live each day as if your
life had just begun.

~ Johann Wolfgang Von Goethe

Date:

Today I choose to...

Evening Reflection:

What surprised me today?

Change your thoughts and
you change the world.

~ Norman Vincent Peale

Date:

Today I choose to...

Evening Reflection:

What did I see today that I'm grateful for?

A man is but the byproduct of his
thoughts. What he thinks, he becomes.

~ Mahatma Ghandi

Date:

Today I choose to...

Evening Reflection:

What is one magical moment I experienced today?

What lies behind us and what lies ahead of us are tiny matters compared to what lies within.

~ Henry Stanley Haskins

Date:

Today I choose to...

Evening Reflection:

What did I feel today that I'm grateful for?

We are shaped by our thoughts;
we become what we think. When
the mind is pure, joy follows like
a shadow that never leaves.

~ Buddha

Date:

Today I choose to...

Evening Reflection:

What was meaningful today?

All action results from thought so it is our thoughts that matters.

~ Sai Baba

Date:

Today I choose to...

Evening Reflection:

Use six words to describe today.

A good life is not lived by chance, but by choice.

~ Kobi Yamada

Date:

Today I choose to...

Evening Reflection:

What is the simplest thing I enjoyed today?

It's not possible. For better or worse, you cannot significantly change your life by manipulating the material world—not by working harder, not by studying longer, not by schmoozing, not by sweating, not by fasting, not by the hair of your chinny chin chin! But change—great change—is inescapable, when you first begin manipulating the world of your thoughts. It is that simple.
~ Mike Dooley

Date:

Today I choose to...

Evening Reflection:

What do I want to remember about today?

The mind moves in the direction of
our currently dominant thoughts.

~ Earl Nightingale

Date:

Today I choose to...

Evening Reflection:

What did I touch today that I'm I grateful for?

Our life is what our
thoughts make it.

~ Marcus Aureluis

Date:

Today I choose to...

Evening Reflection:

What happened today that I wasn't expecting?

We are what we think. All that we are arises with our thoughts. With our thoughts we make the world.

~ Buddha

Date:

Today I choose to...

Evening Reflection:

What brought a smile to my face today?

The soul becomes dyed with
the color of its thoughts.

~ Marcus Aureluis

Date:

Today I choose to...

Evening Reflection:

What gave me a boost today?

The past has no power over us. It doesn't matter how long we have had a negative pattern. The point of power is in the present moment. What a wonderful thing to realize! We can begin to be free in this moment!

~ Louise Hay

Date:

Today I choose to...

Evening Reflection:

What are three thoughts that
made me smile today?

A new state of being creates a new personality ... a new personality produces a new personal reality.

~ Joe Dispenza

Date:

Today I choose to...

Evening Reflection:

I learned something new today ... what was it?

Everything that happens in the
universe starts with intention.

~ Deepak Chopra

Date:

Today I choose to...

Evening Reflection:

What lit me up today?

What the mind can conceive
and believe, and the heart
desire, you can achieve.

~ Norman Vincent Peale

Date:

Today I choose to...

Evening Reflection:

What challenge am I grateful for today?

You are today where your thoughts
have brought you; you will be tomorrow
where your thoughts take you.

~ James Allen

Date:

Today I choose to...

Evening Reflection:

What excited me about today?

Our thoughts and imagination are the only real limits to our possibilities.

~ Orison Swett Marden

Date:

Today I choose to...

Evening Reflection:

What do I want to remember about today?

Thoughts have power; thoughts have energy. You can make your world or break it by your thinking.

~ Susan L. Taylor

Date:

Today I choose to...

Evening Reflection:

What brought me joy today?

Every thought we think is
creating our future.

~ Louise Hay

Date:

Today I choose to...

Evening Reflection:

What made me laugh today?

One small positive thought in the
morning can change your whole day.

~ Unknown

Date:

Today I choose to...

Evening Reflection:

What did I hear today that I'm grateful for?

What consumes your mind
controls your life.

~ Unknown

Date:

Today I choose to...

Evening Reflection:

What did others to see in me today?

Help me to see new ways of being
as I release old ways of seeing.

~ Iyanla Vanzant

Date:

Today I choose to...

Evening Reflection:

What was the source of my strength today?

Be careful what you think. Your thoughts run your life.

~ Proverbs 4:23

Date:

Today I choose to...

Evening Reflection:

What made me feel most alive today?

If you want to experience prosperity at a miraculous level, you must leave behind your old ways of thinking and develop a new way of imagining what is possible for you to experience in your life.

~ Wayne Dyer

Date:

Today I choose to...

Evening Reflection:

What did I do today that brought me happiness?

The happiness of your life depends
on the quality of your thoughts.

~ Marcus Aureluis

Date:

Today I choose to...

Evening Reflection:

What surprised me today?

When we create peace and harmony
and balance in our minds, we
will find it in our lives.

~ Louise Hay

Date:

Today I choose to...

Evening Reflection:

What idea did I have today that I am grateful for?

You only have control over three things in life, the thoughts you think, the images you visualize, and the actions you take.

~ Jack Canfield

Date:

Today I choose to...

Evening Reflection:

What was memorable about today?

As you start to walk out on the way, the way appears.

~ Rumi

Date:

Today I choose to...

Evening Reflection:

What do I cherish about today?

The best way to take care of the future
is to take care of the present moment.

~ Thich Nhat Hanh

Date:

Today I choose to...

Evening Reflection:

In five words or less, who was I today?

Intention leads to behaviors
which leads to habits which
lead to personality development
which leads to destiny.

~ Jack Kornfield

Date:

Today I choose to...

Evening Reflection:

What do I want to remember about today?

It does not matter how long you
live, but how well you do it.

~ Martin Luther King Jr.

Date:

Today I choose to...

Evening Reflection:

What did I see today that made me smile?

What you can do, or dream
you can, begin it; boldness has
genius, power and magic in it.

~ Goethe

Date:

Today I choose to...

Evening Reflection:

What discovery did I make today?

One can make a day of any size
and regulate the rising and
setting of his own sun and the
brightness of its shining.

~ John Muir

Date:

Today I choose to...

Evening Reflection:

What happened today that I did not expect?

Success often comes to those
who dare and act. It seldom
goes to the timid who are ever
afraid of the consequences.

~ Jawaharlal Nehru

Date:

Today I choose to...

Evening Reflection:

What memory from today do I
want to take forward?

You Did It!

You have completed 90 days of intentionally choosing who you want to be and how you want to live. Keep this journal and go back through it, witnessing how you've changed and grown, and remembering the extraordinary journey.

Order a new journal and continue being the creator of your life.

The key to becoming who you want to be is consistency. Stay committed to the practice of choosing an intention and filling the page. Your brain thrives on the daily discipline. You want to keep the joy bubbling and the shifts creating your wonderful, awesome, fabulous life to continue.

If there is ever anything, I can do to support you or add value to your practice, please let me know.

I'm always grateful to connect with like-minded people, so please reach out to me at any time to ask questions, share your experiences or to just say hi.

Visit www.ohmywordjournal.com and check out the community page for inspiration, resources and ways to stay in touch.

One more thing: if OH, MY WORD has added value to your life, I'd love it if you'd help family and friends, become the person they want to be by telling them about it or gifting them a copy of the journal.

Please spread the word.

Thanks so much.

With love and gratitude,

Cheryl

cheryl@ohmywordjournal.com

Acknowledgments

I want to thank the amazing women who agreed to take this OH, MY WORD idea and test it for me. They were not artists nor were they necessarily anxiety sufferers. However, they were open to new adventures.

Every morning they made a decision, *"Today I choose to ..."* and completed the sentence with their intention. They drew the word, coloured it with pencil crayons or gel pens and sometimes added an image or symbol and a splash of glitter. Each one made it uniquely her own.

They took note of their experiences and offered them to me with transparency and openness. My heartfelt thanks to Patricia Asmar, Karen Howes, Karen Regan, Donna McRae and Claire Cilliers. To Lainey Findlay, OH, MY WORD You are amazing.

About The Author

Since learning to say "YES" to unexpected opportunities in her early twenties, Cheryl Wilson-Stewart has walked a variety of paths: television and movie actress, television host, consultant to education and business, speaker and most recently author of the Red Shoe Zone blog, where she helps women navigate the sometimes choppy seas of Life 2.0. and answer the question *"What's next?"* Her passion is helping people to grow and reach their true potential. Cheryl lives in Vancouver, British Columbia. She loves dogs, food and creating almost anything. You can find her at www.ohmywordjournal.com.

About The Illustrator

Claire Moore grew up around improvisation and experimentation. She believes in the benefits of breaking the rules and applies this strategy to her art practice in particular. Originally from Durban, South Africa, she graduated with a Bachelor of Fine Arts from the University of Cape Town and has used it to teach and engage students and communities for most of her adult life. Claire lives in Vancouver, British Columbia, where she has dear friends, a spacious studio and a supportive family. You can find her at www.clairemooreart.com.

CPSIA information can be obtained
at www.ICGtesting.com
Printed in the USA
BVHW042239141020
591019BV00003B/16